Eben Davis

BIOGRAPHICAL SKETCHES

OF

CAPTAIN EBENEZER DAVIS,

AND HIS SON,

THE HON. CHARLES STEWART DAVEIS,

OF PORTLAND, MAINE,

Members of the Massachusetts Society of the Cincinnati.

BY

DAVID G. HASKINS, JR.,
CAMBRIDGE, MASSACHUSETTS.

CAMBRIDGE:
PRESS OF JOHN WILSON AND SON.
1873.

BIOGRAPHICAL SKETCHES.

EBENEZER DAVIS.

Ebenezer Davis or Davies — the name appears in both forms — was born in the little village of Newton, in the south-eastern corner of New Hampshire, about the year 1753. His father was a farmer, who, according to family tradition, removed to some part of Worcester County, Massachusetts. His mother was a Miss Stuart, probably of Scottish descent. He had two younger brothers: William, who served in the Revolutionary war, and afterwards lived in Haverhill, Mass., until his death; and Charles, who died in the West Indies.

The name of Davis was borne by several of the early settlers of Haverhill, from one of whom the subject of this notice was probably descended.

In spite of some little family opposition, Mr. Davis took up arms with the very earliest in the cause of the colonies. The alarm of the memorable 19th of April, 1775, which roused the whole province, called out the minute-men of Bradford, who, under Capt. Nathaniel Gage, marched promptly to the vicinity of Boston, and served seven days. Mr. Davis, who was then living in Bradford, was a private in this company, with which he soon after enlisted in Col. James Frye's regiment of eight months' men from Essex County. The regiment was stationed at Cambridge; and a portion of it, under Lieut.-Col. Brickett, formed a part of the original detachment which, on the night of June 16, under command of Col. Prescott, occupied Breed's Hill, and threw up the famous redoubt. Mr. Davis took part in the conflict of the next day, in which his regiment suffered a loss of fifteen killed and thirty-one wounded.

On the 1st of January, 1776, Mr. Davis seems to have re-enlisted, as a sergeant, under Capt. Joshua Read, in the regiment of Col. James M. Varnum, of Rhode Island. This corps remained with the beleaguering force until the fall of Boston, when it was ordered, with the main body of the army, to New York, and followed the fortunes of Washington through the whole of the checkered campaign of 1776. Mr. Davis was at the battle of White Plains, and also at Trenton and Princeton.

On the 25th of March, 1777, he enlisted as a sergeant under Capt. Samuel Carr, in the 9th regiment of the Massachusetts line, Col. James Wesson, and served in that capacity until March 2, 1779, when he was promoted to the rank of ensign.

He fought at Brandywine and Germantown in 1777,* and in 1778 at Monmouth, where his regiment formed a part of Wayne's brigade in Gen. Lee's command, and Col. Wesson received a severe wound.

On the 1st of January, 1781, the regiment was consolidated with that of Col. Henry Jackson. In the autumn, Ensign Davis was at Yorktown, as assistant commissary of issues to the first brigade of light infantry; a fine corps, which, it will be recollected, did good service in the siege under La Fayette. There is reason to believe that he was

* Col. Wesson's regiment is said to have been at Saratoga with Gates's Northern army, in 1777. The Hon. Charles S. Daveis, however, stated explicitly that his father was at Brandywine and Germantown, and that he was not at Saratoga; and he often reiterated the fact that his father served in every battle in which Washington was engaged. It is not easy now to harmonize these conflicting statements.

at this time attached to the picked regiment of New England light infantry, which, under command of Major Nathan Rice, formed a part of the brigade.

In 1782 we find Ensign Davis on the roll of Col. Michael Jackson's regiment, the redoubtable "bloody eighth." On the 3d of September, 1781, a board was appointed to arrange the rank of the subaltern officers of the Massachusetts line, and in their report he appears as the eighth on the list of ensigns.

On the 15th of March, 1782, he was promoted to the rank of lieutenant. In the following year he was lieutenant in Capt. John Hobby's company of the 3d regiment, Col. Greaton; and by the return of April 16, 1783, he appears as brigade quartermaster. He had thus served his country with credit for eight years, through the whole of her desperate struggle for independence, and had fought in every battle at which Washington had himself been present.

On the conclusion of the war, Lieut. Davis returned to Bradford, where he was married, in July, 1785, to Priscilla, daughter of Deacon Ebenezer and Priscilla (Kimball) Griffin, of that town. At about this time he removed to Portland (then called Falmouth), where he built a house on Free Street, and passed the remainder of his life. His wife died with her infant child; and Mr. Davis, on the 28th of July, 1787, was married at Portland to her younger sister, Mehitable, by whom he had one son, the late Hon. Charles Stewart Daveis, President of the Massachusetts Society of the Cincinnati.

In 1786 Mr. Davis's name appears among the signatures to the petition of the inhabitants of Falmouth Neck for the incorporation of Portland, and that it might be made the shire town. He is said to have been on the committee to name the town, and held several small offices after the incorporation. On the 11th of June, 1798, he was appointed at a town meeting on a committee to "procure labor and materials to erect necessary defences, and to superintend the erection of the same."

Mr. Davis cherished an ardent fondness for military life, and was anxious to take part in the French Revolution. On the 5th of February, 1787, he was commissioned captain in the sixth division of the Massachusetts militia; and a letter is preserved, written by him on the 5th of June, 1798, to Major-Gen. Shepard, then in Congress, asking the influence of the latter with the President to obtain for him a commission in the new army then raising by the government.

He died in the prime of life, on the 14th of November, 1799, aged about forty-six years, exactly one month before his great Revolutionary chieftain. His wife survived him, and on the 7th of November, 1800, was married to John McLellan, of Portland. She died on the 21st of April, 1823, at the age of fifty-five years.

Capt. Davis is described as a man of fine personal appearance and manners, with a military bearing, tall and well proportioned, and, as a young man, athletic and active. He adhered in his dress to the fashions of the old school, — the cocked hat and small-clothes of colonial days. A member of the Federalist party, he steadily supported Washington at the polls, as he had so often done on the field of battle.

CHARLES STEWART DAVEIS.

Charles Stewart Daveis, the only son of Capt. Ebenezer Davis and his wife Mehitable Griffin, was born in Portland, Me., on the 10th of May, 1788.

By his father's early death, in 1799, he was left at the age of eleven years to the care of an excellent mother. After receiving the rudiments of his education in his

Charles S. Daveis

native town, he was sent, in June, 1802, to Phillips Academy, Andover, where, under the instruction of its principal, Mark Newman, he was fitted for college. In 1803, he entered Bowdoin College, then in its infancy, and graduated in 1807, at the head of its second class. As the class at Commencement comprised only three members, each of them was obliged to take two parts, in order to fill up the programme. Mr. Daveis delivered a poem on "Tradition," and a valedictory oration on the "Infirmity of Theory," in the conclusion of which he alluded with much feeling to the recent death of the President, Dr. McKeen.

On leaving college, in Aug. 1807, Mr. Daveis entered the law office of Nicholas Emery, Esq., of Portland; and, after three years of diligent study, was in 1810 admitted to the bar, as an attorney of the Court of Common Pleas. Dismissing some vague thoughts he had entertained of seeking his fortune in the ever-attractive West, he opened an office in Portland, where he remained during the whole of his long professional career.

The bar of Cumberland County was renowned for talent; and Mr. Daveis came into successful competition with very able lawyers, among whom he took a high rank, distinguishing himself by the learning of his legal arguments, and the convincing power of his addresses in jury cases.

While he was well versed in the principles of the Common Law, it was in the less known branches of Equity and Admiralty that he acquired his chief reputation. He was almost the first in the State to devote attention to equity practice, of which the older members of the bar were generally ignorant and distrustful; and his acquirements in this branch were highly esteemed by Judge Story, who was his warm personal friend, and for whom he cherished the strongest admiration. He was an eminent admiralty lawyer, fearlessly espousing, at the risk of his personal safety, the cause of the sailors, who were then regarded when at sea as little better than slaves; a condition of things which he, in conjunction with Mr. Justice Ware, the learned and able Judge of the United States District Court, did much to amend.

On the 1st of June, 1815, Mr. Daveis was married at Exeter, N.H., to Miss Elizabeth Taylor Gilman, youngest daughter of the Hon. John Taylor Gilman, Governor of New Hampshire, and his wife Deborah, daughter of Major-Gen. Nathaniel Folsom, of Exeter.

In 1818, on the election of Samuel Fessenden as major-general of the twelfth division of Massachusetts militia, Mr. Daveis accepted a position on his staff, as division inspector, which he retained until 1827, when, on the accession of his personal friend, Enoch Lincoln, to the office of Governor, he received from the latter an appointment as his senior aide.

It was at this time that he first took an active part in connection with the controversy, with which for many years he was so intimately associated; and of the history, facts, arguments, and condition of which he has been pronounced on good authority to have known more than any other man in the state or nation. This was the dispute relating to the north-eastern boundary of Maine, which had been for many years pending between the United States and Great Britain, but was now suddenly brought to a crisis by the action of the Provincial authorities of New Brunswick, in serving legal process on American settlers in the disputed country; and especially in arresting on his own land, granted to him by the States of Maine and Massachusetts, one John Baker, a citizen of the former State, whom they carried to Fredericton for trial. Gov.

Lincoln promptly despatched Col. Daveis as special agent of the State, bearing a letter to Sir Howard Douglas, the Lieutenant-Governor of New Brunswick, to obtain information with regard to these aggressions, and to demand the release of Baker. Proceeding to St. Stephen's, Mr. Daveis hired horses and a guide, and set out across the country for Fredericton, a distance of over eighty miles, arriving on the 25th of Nov. 1827, after a journey of four days through the wilderness, performed partly on horseback and partly on foot, over miserable roads. The Governor declined to recognize him in an official capacity; but he was treated with the most distinguished politeness, during his stay, by the members of the government, officers, and gentry of the place. After some delay, owing to the Governor's illness, Mr. Daveis proceeded to Houlton and Woodstock, and collected what evidence he was able, in the absence of official recognition, to obtain, in relation to the British aggressions. In January, 1828, he returned to Portland, and on the 31st of that month presented to Gov. Lincoln a report setting forth at length the information that he had acquired on the subject. The mission had proved unsuccessful, and Baker was tried and convicted in spite of all remonstrances.

The controversy, in accordance with the Treaty of Ghent, and by virtue of a convention between the two governments, was now submitted to the arbitration of the King of the Netherlands; and the Hon. Albert Gallatin, and Judge Preble, of Portland, were appointed commissioners to prepare the American case. Judge Preble, who was sent as minister to the Hague, was anxious to avail himself of Mr. Daveis's valuable services in the capacity of Secretary of Legation, an office which the latter declined. He consented, however, on the earnest solicitation of the Judge, to accept an appointment as special confidential agent of the United States, to take charge of the materials of the American case, and to lay them before the arbiter. Sir Howard Douglas, recalled from New Brunswick, was charged by the British government with a similar mission. Mr. Daveis sailed from New York for Havre on the 11th of January, 1830, and on the 13th of March reached the Hague, where he employed himself vigorously in assisting to prepare the case for presentation. After completing his duties here, he made a brief trip to England and Scotland, in the course of which he spent much time attending the courts at Westminster Hall, and the debates of Parliament, and also had the opportunity of making the acquaintance of some of the most eminent men of the period. On the 11th of July he sailed from Liverpool, and reached Boston in safety, after a long voyage.

The unsatisfactory award of the arbiter — being a mere suggestion of a compromise — was not recognized as binding by the United States. The question remained open; and, after some disheartening years of ill-conducted and fruitless negotiation, a bill was at length introduced into Congress, providing for a survey by national authority of the disputed border line. Anxious to secure its passage, the Hon. Edward Kent, at this time Governor of Maine, with the advice of his council, on the 25th of April, 1838, commissioned Mr. Daveis under the great seal of the State as a special agent to co-operate with the Maine delegation in Congress in attaining that result, and also to attend to some other matters connected with the controversy. Mr. Daveis reached Washington on the 10th of May, and devoted himself ardently to the work. The results were eminently favorable. A general interest in the subject was awakened; and, although the bill was laid on the table, resolutions reported in the Senate by the Hon. James

Buchanan were unanimously adopted in both branches, strongly maintaining the right of Maine in the controversy. Of Mr. Daveis's efforts Gov. Kent says: "I think I can confidently say that no agent or envoy ever labored more diligently or more intelligently or efficiently than he did during that warm summer of 1838. . . . By his earnest persuasions, he induced both Mr. Webster (on the 4th of July) and Mr. Buchanan, and others, to espouse our cause distinctly and earnestly, in strong speeches. He alone brought the whole question out of its narrow locality in the State into a national matter, regarded as one of interest to the whole country, involving questions of peace and war, which were fast becoming imminent and perilous. . . . I have always believed that Maine owed more to him than to any other man in thus bringing the whole subject before the nation and compelling action." In a letter addressed to Mr. Daveis, under date of July 15, 1838, Gov. Kent says: "You have breathed into them the breath of life, and have done more to advance our cause, and place this matter on its true basis, and bring the administration to a right position, than any other man has ever done. I am more than satisfied; I am delighted, not more with the success than with the skill and indefatigable and persevering and able manner in which you have presented and enforced our right." Mr. Daveis submitted to the Governor a lengthy and valuable report of his mission, which was laid before the legislature.

The following year, the draft of a convention having been received from England, the Secretary of State, Mr. Forsyth, made a special visit to Maine, to learn the views of the leading men. With this object, at the President's suggestion, Gov. Fairfield and Senator Williams of the dominant party, and Ex-Governor Kent and Mr. Daveis as representatives of the Whig opposition, were invited to a private conference. They met Mr. Forsyth at Portland on the 18th of June, and, after a harmonious consultation for two days, drew up and signed a paper, disapproving the British proposition and the counter-project of the American government, and embodying their own views in the matter.

In 1841, Mr. Daveis, being a member of the State Senate, as chairman of the joint special committee on the North-Eastern Boundary, submitted on the 30th of March an able and dignified report of fifty-five pages, accompanied with a series of resolutions breathing a spirit of calm and unflinching determination, which were adopted unanimously in the Senate, and in the House by a large majority. In May, he was summoned to a private conference on the subject, at Boston, with Mr. Webster, then Secretary of State.

The following year, Lord Ashburton's special mission, resulting in the Treaty of Washington, closed the vexed question for ever. In this last act of the drama, Mr. Daveis took no part. During the long years in which he was identified with the controversy, his feelings had become warmly enlisted on the side of his native State; and he was recognized as one of the most uncompromising and zealous advocates of her right. It was not unnatural therefore that, while acquiescing in the result, he could not give his cordial approval to the terms of settlement.

In politics Mr. Daveis was a Federalist, and afterwards an ardent Whig. Unlike most of his political associates, however, he admitted the justice of the war of 1812. In 1840, he was elected to the State Senate, of which he was an influential member; presiding at its organization, and serving as chairman of the joint special committee on the North-Eastern Boundary, and also as chairman of the joint standing committee on the judiciary. In 1848 he was a warm and active supporter of Gen. Taylor for the Presidency, and was nominated on the Whig State ticket for Elector-at-large, but was beaten by a considerable plurality, the State casting its vote for Gen. Cass.

In the midst of his engrossing public and professional duties, Mr. Daveis never failed to find time for literary pursuits, in which he delighted and excelled. A diligent student, gifted with fine abilities and a rare memory, he acquired an eminent reputation for scholarship, and especially for his familiarity with classical lore. He wrote much, and, in his earlier years, often in verse; and was a frequent contributor to the newspapers and periodicals of the time, including occasionally the "North American Review." He also delivered many public addresses, charming his hearers by the grace of his manner no less than by the beauty of his language. His productions were classical and scholarly, elaborately prepared, and carefully adapted to express the most delicate shades of meaning. His legal studies seem, however, at first, to have left him less time than he could have wished for such pursuits; for in 1809 he writes to his friend, Mr. James Savage, "My Lord Coke has proved almost too much for Dan Apollo, and the charms of *belles-lettres* have been almost lost in the shades of black letter."

His eminent literary abilities were first brought to public notice by an elegant and classical oration on Greek Literature, delivered in Sept. 1808, at Bowdoin College, before the Peucinian Society, of which he had been among the founders; and afterwards published in the Monthly Anthology, prefaced with a most complimentary editorial note. This oration procured him an invitation to contribute to that fastidious publication, and an election as corresponding member of the Anthology Club. Among his other public addresses may be mentioned an oration delivered to the Federal Republicans of Portland, July 4, 1812; a historical oration at Fryeburg, May 19, 1825, on the hundredth anniversary of Lovewell's Indian fight; an oration delivered, at the request of the citizens' committee, on the 9th of August, 1826, on the death of Adams and Jefferson; and a second Fourth of July oration at Portland, in 1831. In 1853 he wrote for the New Hampshire Historical Society a memoir of Gov. Gilman, which was read at Exeter on the hundredth anniversary of the Governor's birth, Dec. 19. On the death of Judge Story, Mr. Daveis drew up a series of beautiful and feeling resolutions, which were adopted at a meeting of the Bar of the United States Circuit Court for the District of Maine, held at Portland, Oct. 1, 1845.

Mr. Daveis was an ardent student of American history, and collected much material for a life of Gen. Knox, which was to have formed one of the concluding series of Mr. Sparks's biographies, and for which the General's family papers were placed at his disposal. Professional duties, however; the extended scope of the work, embracing a sketch of the artillery service during the Revolutionary war; and, finally, an attack of paralysis, — indefinitely postponed the completion of this cherished design, which, though perhaps never formally renounced, remained at last unfulfilled.

To his Alma Mater Mr. Daveis always cherished a strong attachment, and served her faithfully for many years. In 1820 he was chosen a member of the Board of Overseers, of which he was several years Vice-President; and in 1836 he became one of the Trustees, retaining the position until induced by declining health to resign it in 1864. He was a member of the Phi Beta Kappa Society, of which he was for many years Corresponding Secretary, and later Vice-President and President. On the 1st of September, 1835, on the formation of the Alumni Society, of which he was chosen the first President, he delivered an oration, which was highly praised by Judge Story, as "full of strong and vivid thought," and pronounced to "add to his former efforts a new claim upon the gratitude of the scholars of the country." In Sept. 1839, at the inauguration of President Woods, Mr. Daveis delivered a Latin address, which was responded to by the President. He also wrote, for the dedication of the new King Chapel at Brunswick, an able and valuable address on the history of the college, which was delivered on the 1st of September, 1854. In 1844 he received from the college the degree of Doctor of Laws.

Mr. Daveis was in 1828 elected a member of the Maine Historical Society, and was subsequently chosen a corresponding member of the Massachusetts and New Hampshire Societies, and an honorary member of those of New York and Georgia. In 1814 he was chosen an honorary member of the Phi Beta Kappa Society at Harvard College, there being then no chapter of the Society at Brunswick.

In the Massachusetts Society of the Cincinnati, Mr. Daveis always felt the warmest interest, and for many years took a very active part. Elected a member in 1809, at the age of twenty-one years, as successor to his father, he was in 1839 chosen a member of the standing committee, on which he served until 1851, when he was elected Vice-President. In 1853, on the death of Robert G. Shaw, Esq., he was chosen President, and was successively re-elected to that office until his death in 1865. He prepared a new edition of the "Institution and Proceedings" of the Society, which in 1856 was ordered to be printed. He was often chosen delegate to the meetings of the General Society, and in 1854 was elected Vice-President-

General, an office which he retained until his death. In 1859 he wrote for Appleton's Cyclopædia a historical account of the Society. After his death, appropriate resolutions were passed at the General Meeting at Trenton, May 9, 1866, and by the State Society at Boston.

In his active career, Mr. Daveis was suddenly arrested, on the 28th of April, 1850, by a stroke of paralysis, which partially deprived him of the use of his right side. He so far recovered as to be able to resume his ever-busy pen and to mingle once more in society, but he never returned to the practice of his profession. Ten years later, on the 3d of April, 1860, his wife died after a long period of feeble health. Mr. Daveis survived her nearly five years, under the constantly increasing burthen of bodily infirmity, enduring with unmurmuring Christian resignation the inactivity so wearisome to an energetic and social spirit, until the 29th of March, 1865, when, in his native town, on the site of his father's old home, he quietly breathed his last, at the age of seventy-six years.

Mr. Daveis was a man of earnest religious character, the beauty and sincerity of which were amply attested by his whole life, and most of all by the last sad years of feebleness and bereavement, borne with heroic and touching resignation. His faith was unquestioning, and his reverence for sacred and lofty things profound. Of a truly chivalrous nature, he combined in a rare degree manly energy and fearlessness with a womanly tenderness and purity; commanding the sincere respect of all, and the warmest affection of those whose privilege it was to know him well. Though an untiring worker, he always found time to assist those who were deserving of aid, especially young men. His manners were dignified, courtly, affable; and, under whatever provocation, always eminently those of a Christian gentleman. He was not prone to entertain extreme views, and his bearing towards his opponents was ever respectful and courteous.

In social life his conversation sparkled with wit, and with classical quotations and anecdotes, of which he possessed a large fund. He was of middle height, slender and graceful, elegant in figure, and very agile in his movements. Mr. Daveis had five children; namely, —

John Taylor Gilman, M.D., of Portland, an eminent oculist, who d. May 9, 1873.

Edward Henry, a member of the bar in Portland, and editor of some volumes of law reports.

Mary Cogswell, who m. the Rev. David Greene Haskins of Cambridge, Mass.

Anna Ticknor, who m. Charles Jones of Portland.

Caroline Elizabeth, who d. in infancy, Dec. 14, 1827.

www.ingramcontent.com/pod-product-compliance
Lightning Source LLC
LaVergne TN
LVHW011143110826
845150LV00008B/2486
9781418192556